GREAT PAPER CRAFT PROJECTS

Ingrid Klettenheimer

 Sterling Publishing Co., Inc.   New York

Translated by Annette Englander
Edited by Jeanette Green

Library of Congress Cataloging-in-Publication Data

Klettenheimer, Ingrid.
    Great paper craft projects / Ingrid Klettenheimer ; [translated by
Annette Englander].
        p.   cm.
    Portions translated from German.
    Includes index.
    Summary: Provides instructions for making masks, figures, animals,
and other things from paper materials such as paper plates,
cardboard tubes, and coasters.
    ISBN 0-8069-8556-9
    1. Paper work—Juvenile literature.   [1. Paper work.
2. Handicraft.]   I. Title.
TT870.K555   1992
745.54—dc20

        91-43519
          CIP
           AC

10 9 8 7 6 5 4 3 2 1

English translation and editorial arrangement
© 1992 by Sterling Publishing Company
387 Park Avenue South, New York, N.Y. 10016
This book is comprised of portions taken from
the following titles originally published in German
Basteleien mit runder Pappe © 1985 by ALS-Verlag GmbH,
Frankfurt/Main and *Bastelideen rund um die Rolle*
© 1988 by ALS-Verlag GmbH, Frankfurt/Main
Distributed in Canada by Sterling Publishing
% Canadian Manda Group, P.O. Box 920, Station U
Toronto, Ontario, Canada M8Z 5P9
Distributed in Great Britain and Europe by Cassell PLC
Villiers House, 41/47 Strand, London WC2N 5JE
Distributed in Australia by Capricorn Link Ltd.
P.O. Box 665, Lane Cove, NSW 2066
Printed in Hong Kong

Sterling ISBN 0-8069-8556-9

Front cover: Paper Plate Masks in Bright Colors
Back cover: Rooster, Hens, and Chickens

Contents

Introduction

Teachers, parents, and others who enjoy working and playing with children often search for craft projects that are easy and fun. This book contains many paper craft projects that will delight both children and adults. And many of them can be easily created by kindergarten and elementary school children.

For the craft projects in this book, materials are readily at hand. The basic constructions here use cardboard tubes that are usually throwaways and paper plates and cardboard coasters that cost pennies. With a little imagination, these paper products can be transformed into all kinds of characters, animals, puppets, decorations, buildings, and containers.

Paper Plates and Coasters

The round shape of most paper plates does restrict the possibilities of the finished projects, but paper plates are very pliable, so they can be molded a little when wet (with glue) and altered somewhat when dry. And rectangular or square paper plates, often used for cakes, can add variety. Paper plates and coasters can be decorated without any special manual skills. Kindergartners can draw wonderful carnival heads on coasters. Classrooms of children can make masks for Mardi Gras, Halloween, theater play, or just for fun. Add a few ribbons and strings or long sticks, and these paper plate figures become marionettes. Or fold a paper plate in half and you have a fantasy hand puppet with a wide monster mouth.

Make a family of teddy bears, a collection of cats and mice, a barnyard of chickens, a balloon man with a handful of balloons, or a nifty flower bouquet. And paper plates can make fancy hats.

Cardboard Tubes

Start to collect these usual throwaways. Cardboard tubes are even more versatile than paper plates for children's craft projects. All kinds of cardboard tubes come in handy—especially those for toilet paper, paper towels, wrapping paper, yarn, and ribbon. You can also use round boxes that once held baking powder, potato chips, or other sundries. Mailing tubes can be cut down to size as necessary.

Some tubes come colored in a clean white, pink, or brown; so, they may be used just as they are. Others may need to be painted—poster paints work best. You can also cover cardboard tubes with all kinds of paper, cloth, self-adhesive foil, and even wallpaper. It's easy to work quickly and neatly with self-adhesive foils, but they can be expensive for large groups. Some tubes can be hidden inside the body of a particular figure or animal, so you won't have to cover them with paint or paper. Wrapping paper can give a cardboard character a well-dressed look and provide an interesting pattern to flowers, masks, puppets, or animals.

Children will delight in making crocodiles with snapping jaws, finger puppets, fantasy birds, rocking people, stand-up clowns, and windmills as well as many useful containers and even napkin holders for adults. This book even shows you how to build small towns and castles and paper dragons to menace them.

Other Materials

Besides paper plates, coasters, and cardboard tubes, you'll need staples, paper fasteners, paper clips, scissors, glue sticks or white liquid glue, and lots of paints. Crayons, poster paints, and felt-tip markers come in handy for making faces. Crêpe paper, tissue paper, wrapping paper, foil, construction paper, drawing paper, and cardboard in all colors help make the finished projects pleasing. Yarn, cotton wool, and crêpe paper make especially convincing hair. Felt and other fabric scraps, even old manila file folders, and self-adhesive dots help make neat faces and bodies. Barbecue, hors d'oeuvre, and other little wooden sticks; pipe cleaners; cotton balls; and curling ribbons may be useful for some projects.

Templates

Some templates (patterns or stencils) are included in this book for certain projects, like the skiers or crocodiles. Simply trace the pattern on a separate sheet of paper and use that tracing as a pattern that can be passed from child to child. Or trace the template directly onto the kind of paper you plan to use for the finished character or toy, and cut it out. You can alter the size of the template, if you like. Here a photocopy machine that can reproduce copies in various sizes comes in handy. Just make sure you keep everything to scale.

A Word of Caution

Glue sticks are easy to work with, but white liquid glue is usually recommended when working with children since it contains no harmful fumes. Also, any use of spray paint should be supervised by adults.

Exercise care in working with sharp objects and any paints when children are involved.

7

Paper Masks and Faces

Carnival Heads Made from Coasters (p. 7)

Material: Plain round coasters, wide felt-tip pens, hole punch, scissors, curling ribbon, glue sticks, wool leftovers.

The carnival heads on p. 7 were made by kindergarteners. To achieve the mask-like look, stress the eye and mouth parts by surrounding them with color, and also brightly color other facial parts. Before painting the back side, make a hole in the top and bottom of the coasters. Use the top and bottom holes to guide you, so that faces drawn on the opposite side of the coasters do not appear upside down. Wool threads, tied together, braided or twisted, are suitable for designing hair styles. Tie together the finished coasters with curling ribbon in long rows.

Paper Masks from Rectangular Plates (p. 9)

Material: Rectangular cake plates 8¼ by 5¼ inches (13 cm by 20.5 cm) or larger, wide felt-tip pens, pointy scissors, glue sticks, crêpe paper or tissue paper strips.

Kindergarten children also created this piece. Cut openings for eyes, nose, and mouth into the paper plates and paint them with various colors of felt-tip pens. For hair and beard, divide the crêpe paper or tissue paper strips into two to four parts. Fold these lengths in the middle and twist them together in the middle just like the ends of candy wrappers. This way, the tissue or crêpe paper hair becomes firm and it will also stick up out of the head.

Paper Plate Masks in Bright Colors
(p. 10 and cover)

Material: Two paper plates each 7¼ (18.5 cm) or 9 inches (23 cm), opaque paints, water jars and jars for mixing paints, aluminum foil, tissue paper and crêpe paper strips, glue sticks, scissors, thick needles, nylon string.

These masks are dramatic because blues are painted on blue and oranges or reds on orangey red in harmonious shades. First cut openings for the desired facial features into one of the paper plates, and then staple it to the second one. It is easier to first paint the plates with a light color and then to paint patterns and facial features with darker shades. After the colors dry, emphasize individual facial features with rows of small tissue or foil paper balls. Finally, make a wig made from tissue or crêpe paper strips placed together as densely as possible.

Mardi Gras Masks (p. 11)

Material: Nine-inch (23-cm) paper plate, white liquid glue or wallpaper glue, wrapping paper with small patterns, drawing paper, colored construction paper, tissue paper, crêpe paper, pointy scissors, glue stick, aluminum foil, thick darning needles, elastic garters.

Make openings in the plates for eyes, nose, and mouth in the desired places. Fold a three-dimensional nose out of thin cardboard. Then, coat the mask with white liquid glue or wallpaper glue and cover it completely with wrapping paper and decorate with tissue and crêpe paper as well as construction paper scraps. The plate becomes soft and pliable because of the moisture of the glue. The mask can be shaped and dried on a radiator. A wide range of materials can be used to decorate the mask. But it is best to start with the outlines of the eyes and mouth, since their expressions will largely determine the mask's effect.

9   *Paper Masks from Rectangular Plates*

Paper Plate Masks in Bright Colors

Mardi Gras Masks

Easy Cardboard Tube Figures

Figures with Ball Heads   (p. 13)

A nursery school class made the figures shown on p. 13. Wrap cardboard tubes in a small-patterned or solid-colored material, after it has been covered all around with white liquid glue or glue from a glue stick. At the upper and lower edges of the tube, some material will probably jut out. Simply fold it in and attach it to the inside of the tube. For the head form, crumple a piece of newspaper into a ball and cover it with an eight-inch (20-cm) square piece of colored paper, and glue the corners together. Now, coat the upper tube edge with glue and press the ball onto it. Paint facial features on the side with the fewest wrinkles. Make the figure's hairdo and beard out of cotton wool, then add paper hats, buttons, and bows made from scrap material in different colors.

Skiers   (p. 14)

The skiers get big facial features, made from self-adhesive foil or colored paper. For arms, use colored paper strips 5 inches by 1 inch (12.5 cm by 2 cm) folded once and rounded. Attach both sides to the tube with paper fasteners. Then double pieces of crêpe paper, 4¾ inches by 6 inches (15 cm by 12 cm), by folding, and glue them onto the top of the head to form the hats. Gather the crêpe-paper hats with a nylon string. The ski poles can be made out of shortened barbecue sticks or toothpicks. Little round paper disks can be attached to them. Find templates for the skis, ski pole disks, and skier's face below.

SKIER

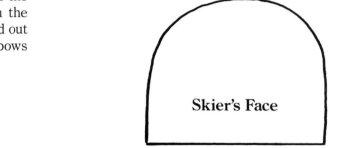

Skier's Face

Ski Pole Disk

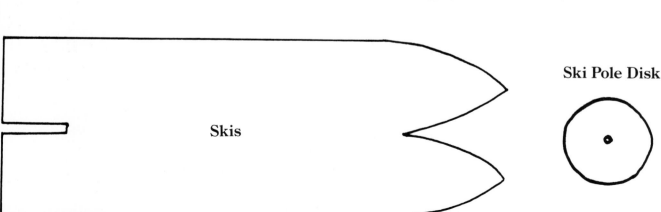

Skis

13 *Figures with Ball Heads*

Skiers

14

15 *Tube Girls with Cardboard Heads*

Tube Girls with Cardboard Heads (p. 15)

The merry group of tube girls on p. 15 is the work of a second-grade class. First paint the facial features on one side of the head shape below, doubled at the top of the head and made out of old file folders or other lightweight cardboard. Paint the back of the head with the desired hair color. After that, unfold the cutout form and glue some crêpe-paper strips in between the front and back head parts. Add more crêpe paper hair to form the forehead curls and the hair at the back of the head. Then, glue the head at its lower, folded neck into the tube; keep it in place at first with paper clips until the glue dries. Add sleeves to the little arms that match the "clothing" that covers the tube before you fasten these arms at the folded ends inside the top of the tube. Depending on the maker's patience and skill, these tube girls can be decorated with belts, bows, or buttons. When working with a school class, it may be useful to prepare a large number of narrow, self-adhesive foil strips and smaller, cut-to-size pieces ahead of time.

Angels (p. 17)

Kindergarten children made the host of angels on the opposite page. Cardboard tubes primed with poster paint form the bodies, and big (2-inch or 5-cm) cellulose balls are used for the heads. First glue together the various parts, then give the angels hair made out of large cotton wool balls, pulled apart a little and arranged. Cut facial features and decorations for the garments out of felt scraps. Also cut the wings out of felt or a folded cloth.

All Kinds of Animals

Material: Two round paper plates the same size; stapler; cardboard for ears and paws; poster paints; thick paintbrushes; water jars; protection base; coasters; glue sticks and white liquid glue; scissors; glossy paper, construction paper, and crêpe paper in bright colors. And for animals that you want to hang up—thick darning needles and nylon strings, and for the goldfish—shiny papers and foils.

Sitting Animals (pp. 19 and 20)

Sitting paper animals include the **Easter Bunnies** on p. 20 and the **Mice** on p. 19. For both the bunnies and the mice, staple together two-thirds of two paper plates and bend the bottom third outward to help form the hind paws, which you then cut out of the paper plate. Give the mice two cardboard circles as ears; the bunnies each get a coaster as a head. Attach long bunny ears made out of colored paper. Also make front paws out of colored paper. Give the animals a coat of poster paint and dry them on top of an egg cup or small glass. The paper plate hind paws help the animal sit up. But you could also stuff the animals with newspapers.

The birds sitting with the Easter bunnies are made out of coasters, supported by cardboard legs—cut from a long rectangle folded up on each side of the bird and with the ends cut into a triangle.

Animals to Hang Up
(pp. 18, 19, 21, and back cover)

In these pages, paper plate animals you can hang up include the **Rooster, Hens, and Chickens** (back cover), the **Teddy Bear Family** below, the **Cats** (p. 19), and the **Goldfish** (p. 21). Their easy creation can be seen from the illustrations. The cat tails are made out of a colored paper spiral, glued onto the back side of the cats. When decorating the goldfish with shiny scales (squamae), it is best to begin at the tail so that you can layer one scale on top of another, just as they are in reality.

Angels

Animals Made from Cardboard Tubes

Caterpillars (p. 22)

Shiny foil strips in different green shades form the patterns of the caterpillar bodies. The end part at the back side is rounded by a 2-inch (5-cm) cellulose ball, painted green and squeezed into the tube. The head is made out of a simple cardboard disk. Paper eyelids and the little snouts may be opened and closed and can be decorated with colorful paper shapes. Be sure to add feelers (antennae). The row of little legs becomes larger toward the head. These little caterpillars like to crawl through the children's room just as much as they do through sand. See the templates on p. 24 for the caterpillar's head, feelers, eyes, mouth, and feet.

Teddy Bear Family

19 *Cat and Mouse Families*

Easter Bunny Family and Birds

20

Goldfish

Shepherd with Sheep (p. 23)

The shepherd with sheep on the opposite page was created by children. A group of children can easily make a nice flock of sheep. For the sheep you will need white toilet paper tubes closed at front and back. Glue circular shapes cut from drawing paper on both sides of the tube to close it. Allow the circles to jut out a little, and cut out indentations so that these can be individually glued onto the tube.

Except for the tail, cut out all copied templates (see p. 24) for the sheep twice. Use drawing cardboard and pay attention to the fold lines. Attach the legs to the ends of the tube. Place the two feet that belong together on top of each other, and immediately press the legs onto the tube with clothespins, until the glue dries. After that, the cardboard legs will have enough tension to support the animal.

Before the head and tail are attached, fold the ends over and coat them with white glue. Then glue the ears onto the head, but fold the larger part outward again. Make the wooly coat of the sheep by gluing on thin strips and layers of cotton wool. A little mouth painted red and eyes made out of dark self-adhesive stickers complete the animals.

The shepherd is made out of two tubes stuck together with the aid of a longitudinal cut. The shepherd's head is a large, painted cotton-wool ball, but wait until you attach his movable cardboard arms with pins or paper fasteners before you glue his head on. Add a thin barbecue stick for his staff.

Caterpillars

23 *Shepherd with Sheep*

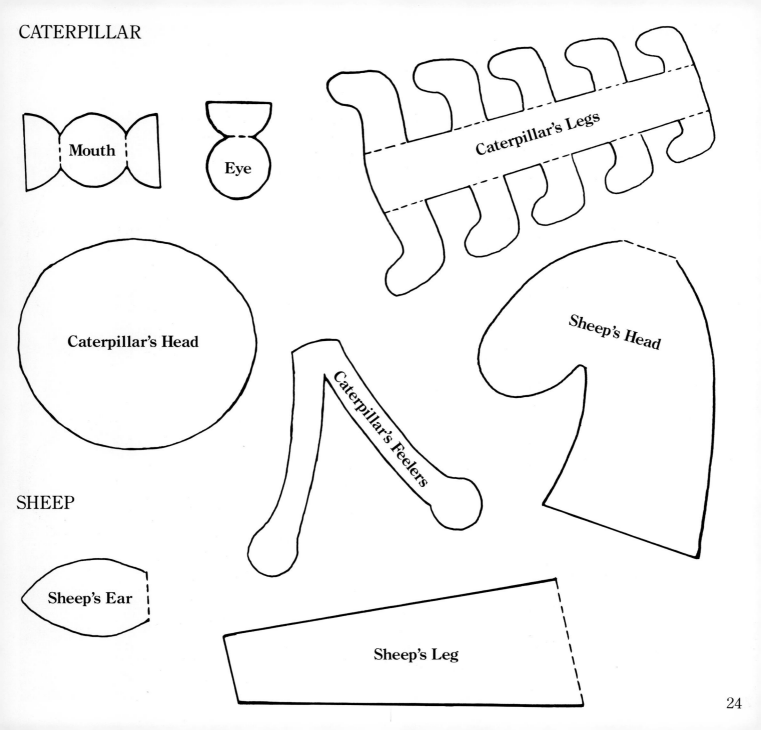

CATERPILLAR

Mouth

Eye

Caterpillar's Legs

Caterpillar's Head

Caterpillar's Feelers

Sheep's Head

SHEEP

Sheep's Ear

Sheep's Leg

DACHSHUND

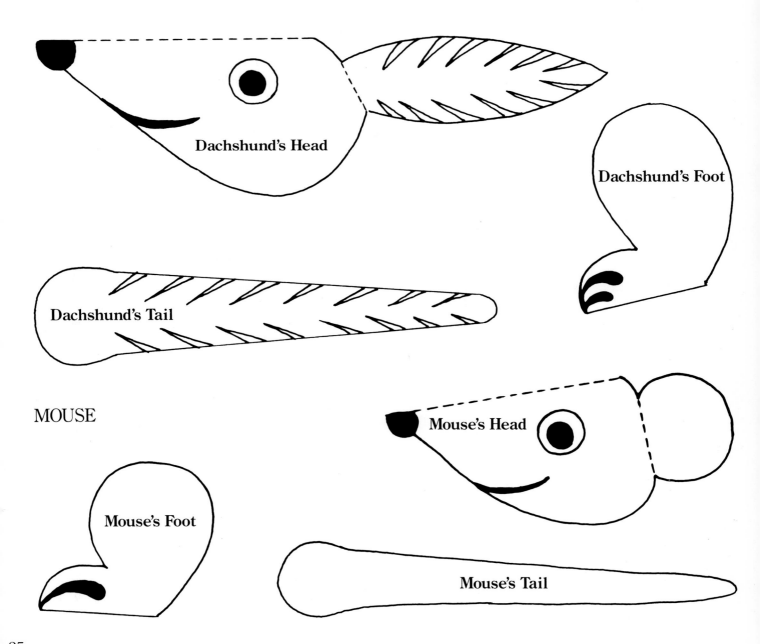

Dachshund's Head

Dachshund's Foot

Dachshund's Tail

MOUSE

Mouse's Head

Mouse's Foot

Mouse's Tail

Dachshunds   (p. 26)

From brown cardboard cut out the four legs, and glue the legs onto the body. Secure parts that you glue onto the tube with clothespins and paper clips until the glue completely dries. While the legs dry, cut out the double-head form with the ears from folded cardboard. Make small, feathery cuts around the edges of the ears. Use self-adhesive stickers for the eyes and tip of the snout. Draw a mouth on both sides with black permanent-ink pens. Last, add the puppy dog tail and cut fringe on both sides of the tail. The tail will curl up after you draw the paper over a table edge. Find templates on p. 25.

Dashing Dachshunds

Mice about a Cheese

Wall Decorations

Ladybugs

Ladybugs   (p. 28)

For the ladybugs, one paper plate represents the body. Cut a second one into two halves and staple the second plate to the first, but leave an open space as shown in the illustration (left on this page) for the wings. The small ladybugs are made out of coasters. Coasters also form the heads of the big bugs. Make holes in the heads of all ladybugs and insert black pipe cleaners for feelers. It's best to paint the individual parts before assembling the whole ladybug.

Turtles   (p. 29)

The turtle shells, made from painted paper plates, sit on a body made from colored construction paper. Elementary school children produced the turtle montage on the page opposite in just three hours.

Flower Bouquet   (p. 30)

The flower bouquet on p. 30 in reds and yellows, made in a fourth-grade class, reveals only at second glance where the beverage coasters are hidden. They are the base of the flower, which is completely covered and then decorated with colorful leaves. Since the heads were first made by the whole class, they turned out all the same size. Since individual parts were pushed together so closely, no gaps had to be filled with leaves or stems.

Balloon Man   (p. 31)

The cheerful chap on p. 31 was made by kindergarten children. They painted the balloon man, who was first stapled together from paper plates and cardboard coasters or disks. The hands and feet were made from disks cut in half. Use a hole punch in the hands and balloons to string the balloons through. Paint the balloon man and the balloons in bright colors with felt-tip pens. The balloon strings are made out of ribbons.

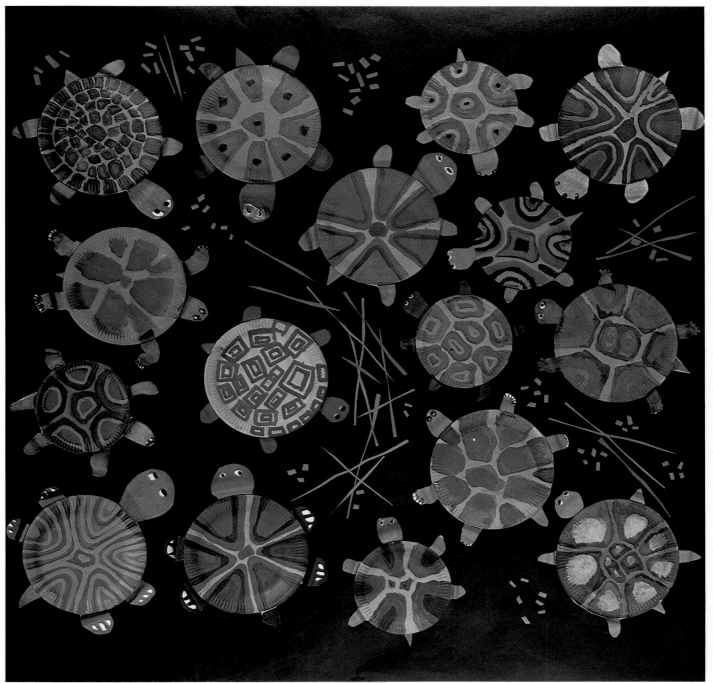

Turtles

Flower Bouquet

31 *Balloon Man*

Stocking Dolls (p. 32)

These easily created little stocking dolls merrily dangle their arms and legs. The arms are clamped into two lateral clefts in tubes covered with shiny paper. They are made out of an individual stocking folded inward to get the desired length. Before both ends are tied together, the stockings are filled with a small cellulose ball. Tie a whole pantihose at the pantyline and tie it once more underneath a ball so that one side can be pulled up smoothly to create a face. After the stocking legs have been threaded through the tube on both sides past the arms, the feet can be folded in like the arms and made bigger with the aid of a cotton-wool ball. Finally, a painted ball is stuck into the tube between the legs to prevent the legs and upper body from sliding out. Make facial features out of felt leftovers to complete the stocking figure. The part of the pantihose that sticks out above the head can be shaped into various hairstyles or caps.

Stocking Dolls

Men and Boys Fit for Hanging

The basic structure for the **Snowmen** (p. 35), the **Coaster Puppets** below (p. 33), the **Funny Clowns** (p. 34), and the **Tall Streaks** and **Fat Bellies** (p. 37) is much the same. Usually two paper plates or two coasters the same size are stapled together. Then you can decorate them however you wish. For the Coaster Puppets, beverage coasters or round disks form both head and body. The limbs are simply coasters cut apart. The puppets were covered with wallpaper (wrapping paper will work) and the head and limbs are movable since paper fasteners join them to the trunk. Paper cutouts make the facial features. The Tall Streaks are made from coasters attached with curling ribbon strung through holes made by a hole punch. Their arms and legs are made out of strips of colored paper braided in cat springs or witch's steps and glued onto the cardboard disks. Faces are drawn with felt-tip pens or with paper cutouts. The Fat Bellies' hair can be glued on. Crêpe-paper strips are made into curls and pulled apart slightly to form the desired hairstyle.

Coaster Puppets

Funny Clowns

Pippi Longstocking (p. 36)

Paint the tube bodies and decorate them with glossy paper strips. Make arms and legs out of long cat springs or witch's steps (see directions on this page). Then glue the ends together and attach them with four paper fasteners. Cut shoes and hands out of colored paper. Use large cotton balls for heads and draw on a freckled face with permanent pencils. Add Pippi's red braids with crêpe paper. The Pippi Longstocking dolls shown below were made by second-graders.

Cat Springs or Witch's Steps

To make the cat springs or witch's steps, fold together two long, narrow strips of paper the same length. You can make both strips out of the same paper or choose two different colors. Just make sure the paper is not too thin. First, place strip A at a 90° angle to strip B; then fold B from left to right over A. Now fold A over B in the same way—always fold the upper strip over the lower. Continue folding the two strips, and the finished garland will have a springy, step-like appearance.

Pippi Longstocking

Tall Streaks and Fat Bellies

Reversible Cinderella Doll   (p. 38)

The reversible doll shown below illustrates both the sad, tearful Cinderella and the released, happy Cinderella. Make the head out of large cotton-wool balls, primed with poster paint, a cloth skirt cut in a circular shape about 8 inches (20 cm) in diameter, and two cloth strips from the same fabric as the skirt 1½ inches by 7 inches (4 cm by 18 cm) for the arms. Both figures have the same covered cardboard tube for the torso.

Make two small cuts in both ends of the tube. Then fold the fabric for the arms into three layers and glue the fabric together and tie it at each "hand" end. You'll be making two sets of arms. Insert one pair in the top of the tube and the second in the bottom. Push the cardboard tube through a hole in the middle of the cloth circular skirt (measured tightly) and glue the skirt to the tube in the middle. Attach the heads on both sides of the tube above the arms. Draw a crying face on one head and a

Reversible Cinderella Doll

38

laughing, happy face on the other. Attach hair made of wool or hemp. Give the freed, happy Cinderella jewelry and a little crown made out of braid leftovers. When playing with the doll, the arms of the covered-up figure show from underneath the skirt as though they were legs. Be sure to remember to use the glossy "right" side of the skirt fabric for the happy Cinderella and its dull underside for the unhappy girl.

Clown Family (p. 39)

These clowns are created just like the clowns with wobbly arms, with a few additions. Carefully cut out hands and large shoe forms from the patterns on p. 40. Set the large clown heads on early Victorian collars and add red cotton-ball noses. Add bright hair made out of excelsior or Easter basket grass, little hats made of cotton-wool cones, and pipe-cleaner bows to decorate them. The tall

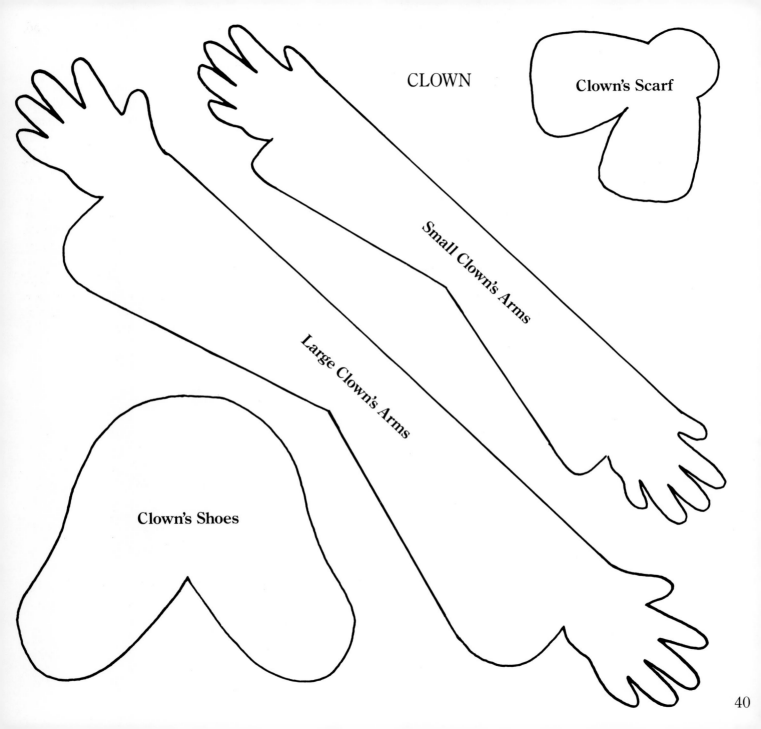

CLOWN

Clown's Scarf

Small Clown's Arms

Large Clown's Arms

Clown's Shoes

40

clowns' bodies are made from two tubes stuck together. Make a slit into the lower tube to join them. They also have large heads and noses. Paint on facial features with permanent pens.

Clowns with Wobbly Arms   (p. 42)

It is easy to make these clowns with wobbly arms. Make vertical cuts up to the middle in a covered cardboard tube; this will allow the arms to move freely. Follow the pattern on p. 41 for the arms. Cut them out of colorful cardboard, and punch them in the middle with the hole punch. Punch two larger round holes opposite each other into the tube above the center. Stick a barbecue stick through the tube from behind to the front, catching the inside middle of the "arms." The stick can turn in the tube, and since it tightly holds the cardboard arms, it allows them to swing up and down. Decorate the front of the wooden stick with a bow tie (see pattern on p. 40) and glue on a wooden bead. If the wooden stick juts out too far

in back, shorten it. Use a cotton-wool ball for the head. Prime the clown's face with a skin color and decorate head and body with felt leftovers and permanent ink.

Windmills   (p. 43)

If you've collected brown toilet paper tubes, you do not need to paint them. Simply draw windows and doors on the tubes with felt-tip pens for the windmill towers. Make the arms of the windmill out of 4-inch (10-cm) squares of drawing paper. Cut the square diagonally almost up to the middle. When every second corner has been glued on, punch holes into the middle. Also punch two holes in the tower. Feed a strong flower wire through the holes. Bend the end of the wire inside the tube and run it through the arms of the windmill. Use a bead to hold the windmill arms in place and bend the wire once more to secure the bead. With just a small puff of wind, the little windmill's arms rotate. Last, add a cone-shaped roof.

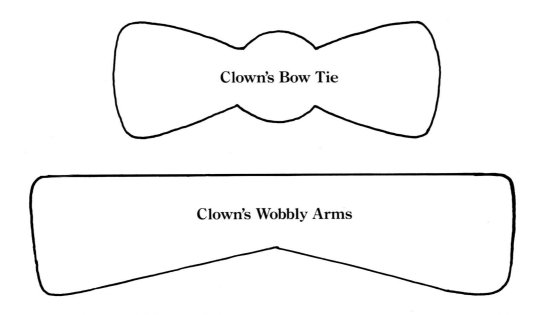

Clown's Bow Tie

Clown's Wobbly Arms

Clowns with Wobbly Arms

Windmills

Floating Birds   (p. 44)

For the floating birds, trace both bird-wing stencils on p. 45 onto two similar colors of construction paper. Cut them out of the construction paper and glue them together in the middle only. Then glue the larger wing underneath the tube, so that its ends are flush with the tube. Use paper clips to secure the spots where the wings are glued on. Let the wings dry. Paint a cotton-wool egg 2¼ inches (10.5 cm) in diameter the same color as the tube. Insert it into the tube to form the head. Use self-adhesive stickers for the eyes and use colored construction paper to cut out the beak from the pattern on p. 45. Attach the beak on both sides at the tip of the head. Use eight strips of paper ¾-inch (2-cm) wide for the tail. (Match the wing color.) Set the tail "feathers" apart slightly and attach them to the inner side of the tube. Curl them with scissors. Hang them by a string attached between the wings under a colored paper strip that's as long as the body.

FLOATING BIRD

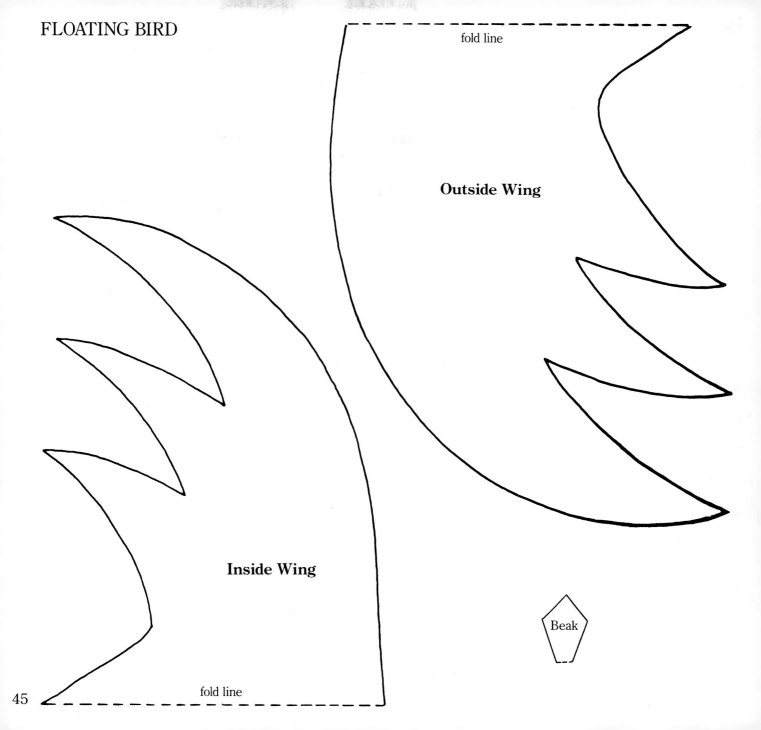

fold line

Outside Wing

Inside Wing

Beak

fold line

45

Rocking People (p. 47)

Turn a little more than half a cardboard tube cut length-wise into a seesaw. In small cuts at the edge, insert little painted cardboard people (see template below) which can be painted with colored pencils and felt-tip pens and be as varied as you choose.

Flying Witches (p. 44)

The flying witches on p. 44 can be created by small children, with a little help. Punch a hole into the upper edge of the cardboard tube and pull a nylon string through and tie it. Push two long 14-inch (35-cm) pipe cleaners through two more holes and attach the pipe cleaners to a painted cotton-wool ball head 2¼ inches (6 cm) in diameter. Be sure the nose side faces forward. Glue a small ball ½ inch (1.5 cm) in diameter into a small opening in the large ball. Create the witch's skirts with double-layered crêpe paper that's 4 inches by 3½ inches (10 cm by 8.5 cm). Gather them together and cover the seam with a foil strip belt. The broomstick is a 12-inch (30-cm) long, round wooden stick (4 mm in diameter), and wind the pipe cleaner ends, which become the witch's hands, around them. Decorate the rear end of the stick with a crêpe-paper tassel and push the stick through two more holes in the tube. Then attach the witch's hair made out of cut and arranged crêpe paper to the head. Use the stencil below for the kerchief. Be sure to fold over a small rim at the front edge, as shown, before you glue it on.

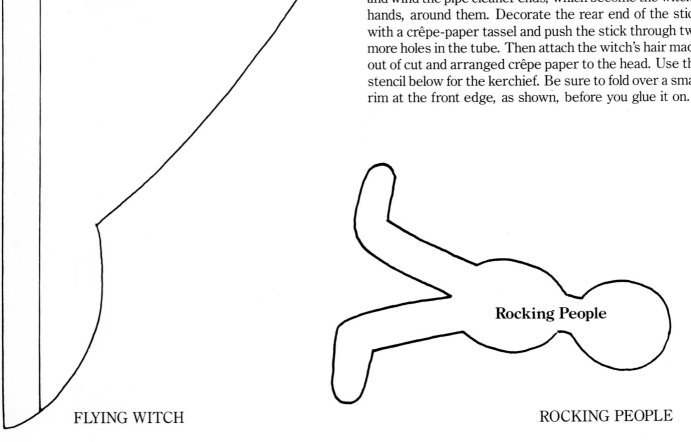

Flying Witch's Kerchief

Rocking People

FLYING WITCH

ROCKING PEOPLE

Rocking People

Flying Witches

49 *Egg-Carton Marionettes*

Theater

Material: Assorted paper plates, coasters, poster paints, paintbrushes, water jars, protection bases, scissors, white liquid glue, glue sticks, colorful foil, crêpe paper, white drawing paper, file-folder cardboard, stapler. For the stick figure puppets, long pinewood strips. For the egg-carton marionettes, egg cartons, yarn or thin string, thick darning needles, little sticks to guide them. For the circus director with animals, rectangular paper plates, paper fasteners, nylon string, drawing paper, string, strong cardboard strips. For the hand puppets, spray paint, white Styrofoam balls, sharp kitchen knife.

Egg-Carton Marionettes   (p. 49)

These simple marionettes with movable hands (see p. 49) are made of covered coasters and pieces of egg cartons, strung up alternately, imitating the skeleton and moving body parts. For the head, use the cardboard disk vertically; cover it with colored paper and complete it with glossy paper for hair and facial features. Make arms and legs out of strung egg-carton pieces. Cut the hands and feet out of paper-covered cardboard disks. Attach three strings—one for the head and one for each hand. To hold the figure up, tie these strings to a little stick. And your egg-carton marionette is ready to introduce itself.

Hand Puppets   (p. 51)

These hand puppet animals and monsters are easy to make. Round paper plates are so flexible that after they're bent in the middle, they open up again. This attribute is useful for simple play figures.

Glue or carefully staple the outer rim of a painted half plate to another painted plate so that your hand can fit inside to open and close the hand puppet's mouth. The fastest and easiest way is to spray-paint the inside and outside of the plates. As eyes, cut Styrofoam balls into halves or quarters. But drawing cardboard could also be used for eyes; double it to cut out the two eyes. Make ears, teeth, and tongue out of drawing or colored paper to complete the scurrilous heads.

Circus Director with Animals   (p. 52)

First paint the back sides of two rectangular paper plates for each animal and connect them as loosely as possible. Also connect four thigh and four lower-leg parts of the same size each—also made out of painted cardboard. Cut out leg parts of equal size by placing one cut form atop the matching leg part. Use paper fasteners where the legs bend and where they attach to the body (see the illustration on p. 52). Now you can staple the two body halves together. Fasten the cutout head to the body with a short cat spring (witch's step) made from drawing paper strips. The head will wobble with each movement. A string tied to the front and back of the body is also strung through a strong cardboard strip which, during play, acts as the bar guiding the puppet.

Stick Figures   (p. 53)

Staple two plates together to create the belly and glue a long pinewood stick inside. There are many possibilities for designing these figures. Let the illustration on p. 53 help stimulate your imagination.

Hand Puppets

Circus Director with Animals

52

Stick Figures

Marionette Birds

Marionette Birds (p. 54)

To make the marionette bird's neck, string a row of little tissue-paper balls, and crown them with a painted cotton-wool ball head about 1½ inches (4 cm) in diameter, and last, glue on a little paper ball. A 40-inch (1-m)-long string can be tied up and pulled through the tissue balls and head as well as through the front edge of the tube. Add stickers for eyes and a colored paper beak. Cut out triangular, accordion-shape folded wings from colored paper, using the pattern on p. 57. Pull a long (20-inch or 50-cm) pipe cleaner through two holes on the tube body's underside. Bend the pipe cleaners to form feet. Create a tail with colorful feathers and glue it to the inside of the tube. A string through both the head and rear body of the marionette bird allow you to animate it.

Finger Puppets

Fairy Tale Characters (p. 56)

These simple fairy tale characters are made in essentially the same way as the group of girls with cardboard heads on p. 15—except the body tubes are shortened to 3¼ inches (8 cm). And instead of the girls' glued-on arms, make two round openings a little below the middle of the body front. Place fingers through the holes to act as the figures' arms. Decorate the figures with colorful crêpe paper and construction paper. Small, white self-adhesive dots (⅓ inch [8 mm]) work for eyes, and faces may be drawn with felt-tip pens or colored pencils. Just use patience and imagination. (Use the head template on p. 16.)

Fantasy Birds

These exotic birds are quickly crafted out of toilet paper tubes that are cut into halves. Two round openings allow children to stick their thumbs and forefingers through, when playing. In this way, they will be able to clack their fingers together, like a beak. Make large eyes with self-adhesive foil, and add wing shapes (see template on p. 57) out of colored paper to cover up the places where larger, real feathers are glued on.

Tube Dragons

These dragons, made out of tubes covered in green, have pointy cut-ins on both sides, decorated with white pointy teeth rows. Glue a large, bent, red paper tongue to the inner underside of the tube. And decorate your dragons with shiny foil eyes and a spiky mane. A hole at the dragon's rear underside allows fingers to animate the dragon. The back part of the body is made out of leaf-shapes cut into crêpe paper, which covers up the guiding hand.

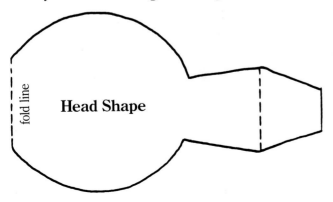

fold line

Head Shape

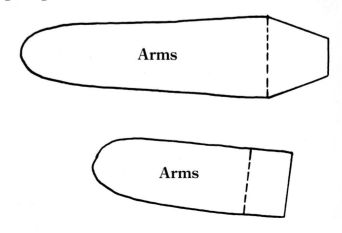

Arms

Arms

Fantasy Birds

FANTASY BIRD

Bird's Eyes

Marionette Bird's Wings

Feathers

MARIONETTE BIRD

Tube Dragons

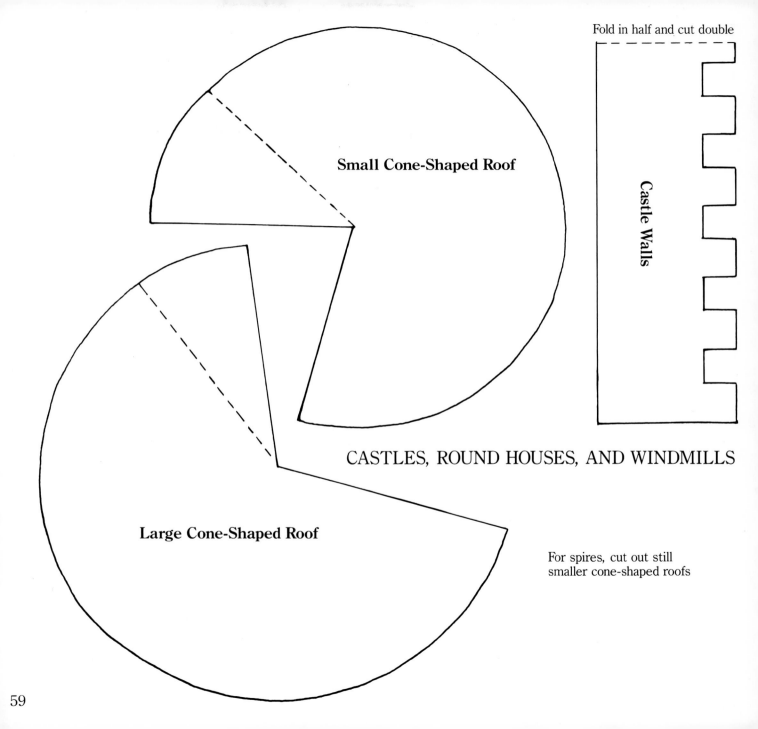

Small Cone-Shaped Roof

Fold in half and cut double

Castle Walls

Large Cone-Shaped Roof

CASTLES, ROUND HOUSES, AND WINDMILLS

For spires, cut out still
smaller cone-shaped roofs

Building Castles in the Air

Knight's Castle   (p. 61)

Cardboard tubes in all sizes can be put together quickly to make a large knight's castle. Since two parts are connected by wall pieces, you can vary the look of the castle and add to it later. Tower crowns with loopholes (crenellations) made of brown cardboard and cone-shaped roofs for the smaller tower will make it look real. Draw small windows high up, and Roman-arch doorways cut out of colored paper or shiny, dark brown, self-adhesive foil. See two templates for cone-shaped roofs on p. 59 and crenellations for towers on this page (p. 60) and castle walls on p. 24. Add tab ends to these walls (as shown on p. 61) to attach one tower to another.

Fairy Tale Castle   (p. 62)

Luminous pinks and glittering foil make this fairy tale castle a delight. Turn a large rectangular and a small square box into the main castle building, surrounded by little and big towers of all sizes. The towers are created with tubes from aluminum foil rolls, toilet-paper rolls, and the inner spools of yarn and ribbon. They are all covered with light pink shiny foil that makes them all go well together. Glimmery crowns are the cone-shaped roofs (see patterns on p. 59); they shine in shades of pink and red. Windows are made of construction paper and doors from glittery self-adhesive foil. The tall tree trunks are also covered with shiny foil; bundles of green transparent paper, cut into created leaf shapes, are stuck inside the trunks as tree tops. This castle can also be expanded any way you like. It could also be inhabited by little paper dolls.

Building with Tubes

Round Houses   (p. 64)

These cardboard tubes make attractive round houses, covered with white self-adhesive foil. Most were the inner spools of yarn, braid, and ribbon. Windows, doors, and flower boxes can be made quickly out of self-adhesive shiny foil pieces. Or they could be made of construction paper and stuck on with white liquid glue. Make small windows inside larger window frames. Use the cone-shaped roof patterns on p. 59.

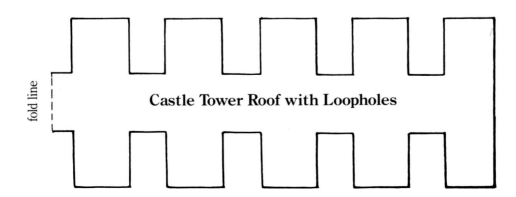

fold line

Castle Tower Roof with Loopholes

61 *Knight's Castle*

Fairy Tale Castle

Little Bird Houses

Little Bird Houses   (p. 63)

A small white paper plate, three square coasters and a white toilet-paper tube form this little bird house. The basic construction is easy except for the triangular roof, because the square disks can easily slide off before they are glued, taped, or stapled together. Children can make little birds from small and big rings with wide, colored paper strips. Glue the two rings together to create the bird's head and body. The piece that juts out of the larger ring can be cut into a tail shape. For wings, glue another piece of colored paper to the back. Make the beak out of a triangular-shaped form which can be cut, folded over and doubled. Attach the little birds to the roof and to the plate around the tube. Glue on birdseed to make the bird houses look even more real.

Round Houses

Crocodiles   (p. 65)

Kindergarten children can make these crocodiles shown on the opposite page. First trace the crocodile patterns on pp. 66 and 67 out of green construction paper. The cardboard tube between the two crocodile shapes is painted green and glued on. Then cut long, folded white paper strips in a zigzag pattern for the crocodile's teeth, and glue them into the mouth. Make the eyes out of white and black glossy paper bent upward. For some texture, roll up little green tissue-paper balls for the crocodile's back. Now pull a nylon string through the crocodile's upper and lower jaws. Knot it tightly, and run it through the tube and tail diagonally opposite. When children pull the string, the crocodile snaps its mouth.

Crocodiles

CROCODILE

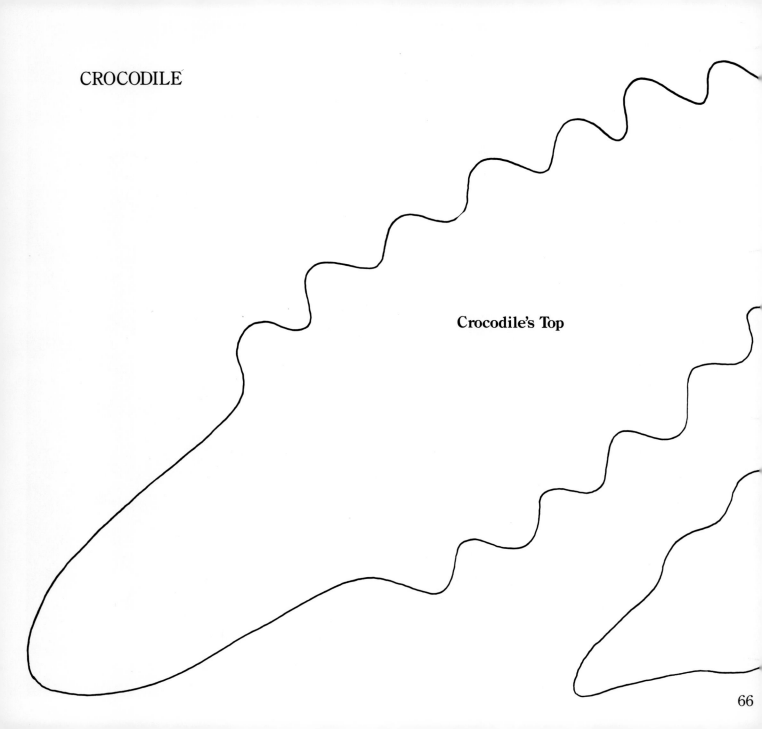

Crocodile's Top

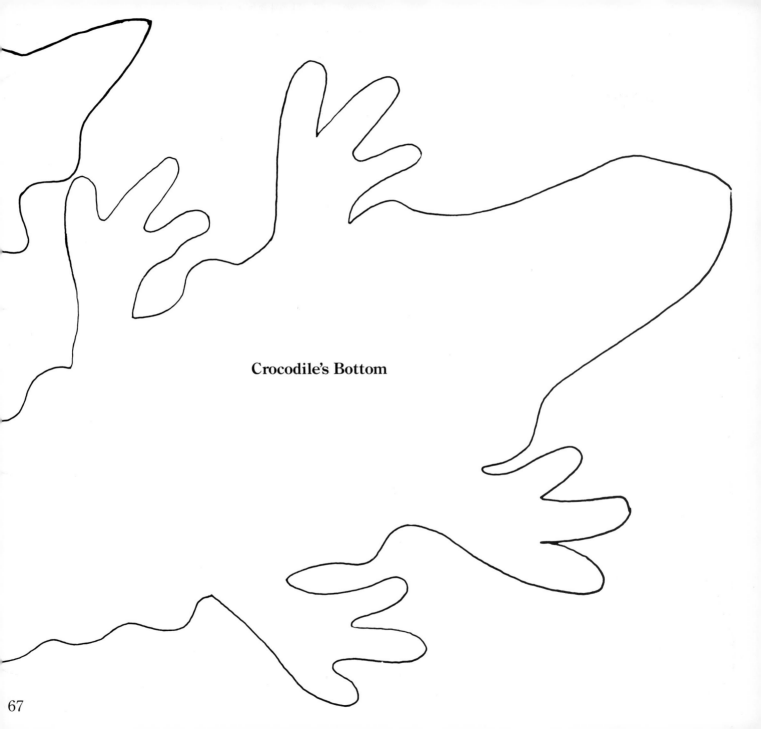

Crocodile's Bottom

67

Fancy Flower Hats

Flowers Blooming Everywhere

Paper Plate Flowers   (p. 69)

Material: Two 7¼-inch (18.5-cm) paper plates, colored tissue papers, glue stick or white liquid glue, green construction paper, leaf pattern, pencil, scissors, green curling ribbon.

First cut out a large green circular leaf shape (see illustration on this page) from colored construction paper, and place the cutout leaves between two paper plates. Glue the plates together back to back, allowing the paper leaves to stick out around the rim. Then cover one or both sides of the paper plates with colored tissue-paper balls. It may be easier to cover the plate with glue first, before attaching the balls. Use curling ribbon to hang up the flowers.

Fancy Flower Hats   (p. 68)

Material: Nine-inch (23-cm) paper plates, green spray paint or poster paint, green construction paper for leaves, wide crêpe-paper strips, white liquid glue, thick needles, elastic garters or pony-tail elastic bands, stapler.

Use green paper plates or paint the outside rim green and place a construction paper leaf rosette on top. Attach more crêpe paper leaves or petals for the flowers. Crêpe-paper flowers can be made out of rolled-up strips cut in the petal shapes. In the wide center, the flowers are held together with staples or gathered with an elastic band and closely attached with glue.

Paper Plate Kids   (p. 70)

For the paper plate kids, make their figures out of two paper plates the same size and staple them together halfway. Then fold the two lower parts out. Make arms and legs out of file folders or cardboard, or paint in the desired skin tone. Decorate coasters for the heads. These paper plate boys and girls can make attractive table decorations that will tickle children.

69

Paper Plate Flowers

Decorator Plates

Round Weavings   (p. 73)

Material: Paper plates in different sizes, scissors, wool and yarn leftovers, thick knitting needles, scissors, tape.

This textile craft will help you introduce weaving to children. The round weavings can be put together into a large montage of wall pictures, or you could add construction-paper stems and leaves to make them into flowers.

First make cuts around the rim, leaving ¾- to 1¼-inch (2- to 3-cm) spaces in between, and make sure that you give the plate an even number of cuts. Stretch threads across the inside of the plate in the shape of a star, and glue them down. Begin weaving in a circle, starting in the center and gradually moving outward. Use yarn or wool leftovers.

Flower Bouquet Plates   (p. 73)

Material: One 9-inch (23-cm) and one 7¼-inch (18.5-cm) paper plate, white drawing paper, pointy scissors, colorful spray paints, glue sticks or white liquid glue, pencils, pins, newspapers to protect against paint spills.

Trace a small paper plate on drawing paper; cut out the circular shape and fold it in the middle. On one side, draw half of a flower bouquet, cut it out of folded, doubled paper, and unfold the cut and finished design. Working on a newspaper base, pin the flower bouquet cutout with many pins onto the inside of a large plate. Spray-paint it with the desired color. After it has dried, detach the paper cutout from the plate. Now you can hang up both the spray-painted plate and a second plate with a cutout as wall decorations.

Tissue-Ball Plates   (p. 73)

Material: Small paper plates, tissue paper, glue stick, ribbon, transparent tape.

The plates with tissue-ball designs were made much like the paper-plate flowers on p. 69. These tissue-ball designs require a single plate and no construction-paper leaves. Coat the inside of a small paper plate with glue and press the small tissue-paper balls onto it. The plates look best with flower-shaped designs. Hang the finished plate by a ribbon.

Note Holders   (not shown)

Material: Two paper plates (in different colors if possible), scissors, stapler, colorful spray paint, colored construction-paper leftovers, crayons, thick darning needles, white liquid glue or glue sticks, ribbon.

Note holders can hold Christmas cards, Easter greetings, or New Year's resolutions. They make a nice wall decoration and are suitable presents to take to a friend as a small gift. Add whatever designs you like. To create the basic shape, take a whole paper plate and a second one cut in half. Then attach them with glue, forming a pocket. It's easier to paint the paper plates (if they're not already colored plates) before they are attached to each other. Use a piece of newspaper as protection. Decorate the note holder with motifs cut out of colored paper, paint them, or color them with crayons.

73 *Flower Bouquet Plates and Tissue-Ball Plates*

Tube Containers

Round Containers (p. 74)

Cover tubes of different sizes with foil to hold all kinds of little things. Glue the tube onto a round cardboard paper bottom. (Trace the tube for the right size.) For a finished look, fold the foil in at the upper edge a little. If you like, glue several short tubes onto a large, round cardboard circle (see the illustration below). These containers are especially nice for holding office or work desk supplies.

Savings Banks (p. 75)

Larger tubes with bottoms and lids, such as mailing tubes or tubes for potato chips can be turned into droll savings banks. With a pointy knife or scissors, cut a mouth slit that will act as the opening for coins in the savings bank. Cover up uneven edges with a mouth cut from self-adhesive foil or construction paper. Cut out a nose and large eyes from various colored foils. For the tufted hairstyles, cut many strips of an unopened crêpe-paper roll, tie them together on one end with a string, then glue them tightly together on the lid. Finally, give your banker a haircut to create the desired hairstyle.

Bear Containers (p. 76)

Cut little bears out of cardboard. See the pattern on p. 77—use a photocopy machine to enlarge the bear to a suitable size to hold the tube container. Draw a face and paw marks on the bear as shown. Cover a broad tube with foil, or decorate it as you wish. These bear containers make nice party favors for children. You can fill them with candy or other goodies.

Round Containers

Savings Banks

Bear Containers

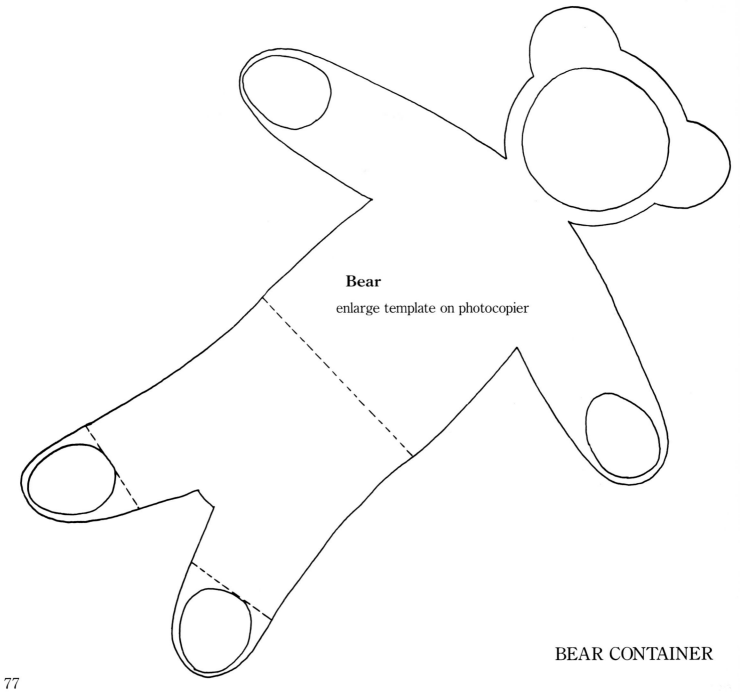

Bear

enlarge template on photocopier

BEAR CONTAINER

77

Napkin Holders

Bird Napkin Holders (p. 78)

For these bird napkin holders, shorten cardboard tubes to 2½ inches (6 cm) long, and glue on smaller tubes 1½ inches by 5¼ inches (4 cm by 13 cm) as heads. Make eyes out of self-adhesive stickers, and the headdress out of curled ribbon, pulled through two closely placed holes at the top of the head. Make the head, feet, and tail from cardboard the same color. A long cardboard strip 1½ inches by 10 inches (4 cm by 25 cm) should be folded in half and cut into tail feathers at one end and into toes at the other. Unfold the strip and glue it to the underside of the bird's body. Add a napkin folded in a triangle and inserted into the tube for wings.

Flower Napkin Holders (p. 79)

These flower napkin holders are made from cardboard tubes covered in shiny green paper. Glue a painted wooden spatula deep inside the tube. Fold foil paper so that you have three layers, and cut out circular flower shapes. Make the large, outside circles of petals 5¼ inches (13.5 cm) in diameter, the second 3¼ inches (8 cm), and the third 2½ inches (3 cm). Two identical flowers decorate each side of the spatula. Fold a green napkin diagonally in accordion folds; bend it in the middle and push it into the cardboard tube to form the leaves. Since so many individual parts must be made for one flower, these napkin holders take time. But the flowers—perhaps made in colors to match your china—can be used over and over again.

Bird Napkin Holders

79 *Flower Napkin Holders*

Index